फीलिंग्स ऑफ़ हार्ट

शुभांजली निषाद

क्रम-सूची

क्रम-सूची

क्रम-सूची

भूमिका

"Feelings of Heart", which is an Anthology book set on the feelings of the heart, which is written with the help of 30 co-authors. All about having a feeling for someone, but do not know to share our feelings, or may be we feel shy or feel affraid of loosing someone we love so much . we want someone in our life forever and fell so broken only by thinking of losing them them, we leave our own self broken from inside out .

अस्वीकरण

इस संकलन में पब्लिकेशन ने ये सुनिश्चित किया है की प्रत्येक रचाएं लेखकों द्वारा स्वरचित हैं । इस पुस्तक में लिखी प्रत्येक कविताएं ,शायरी , पत्र लेखकों द्वारा स्वरचित है यदि इसके बाद भी किसी रचना की चोरी पाई जाती है तो इसके ज़िम्मेदार हम नहीं स्वय लेखक होंगे । हमने सभी लेखकों से स्वरचित एवं अप्रकाशित रचनाओं के लेखन की माँग की थी । हमारा संबंध निष्कपट एवं विश्वास पर आधारित है ।

संपादक

पावती (स्वीकृति)

सर्वप्रथम मैं कृष्णा जी के समक्ष नमन करती हूँ । जिनकी कृपा से हमारी ये किताब निर्विघ्न रूप से संपन्न हो सकी । उसके बाद मैं अपने माता - पिता का भी दिल से शुक्रिया अदा करती हूँ उन्होंने मेरा साथ हमेशा दिया और मेरा प्रोतसाहन बढ़ाया ।

Words of soul Publication के संस्थापक निकिता दुदगी जी , को - संस्थापक लक्की पाण्डेय जी एवं सभी सदस्यों का दिल से शुक्रिया अदा करती हूँ । जिन्होंने मुझपर अपना विश्वास बनाए रखा और इस सफर में हमारा हौसला बढ़ाया एवं इस संकलन को सफलतापूर्वक पूरा करने में मेरा साथ निभाया । हमने किताब में सभी आवश्यक परिवर्तन और बहारी आवरण को खूबसूरत बनाकर किताब को और आकर्षक बनाने का प्रयास किया है ।

अंत में मैं अपने " Feelings of Heart" के पूरे परिवार को दिल से शुक्रिया करती हूँ जिनके बिना इस किताब का सपना पूरा करना नामुमकिन सा था और अपना बहुमूल्य समय और सहयोग दिया । साथ ही साथ हमारे ऊपर अपना विश्वास भी बनाए रखा और धैर्य के साथ हर पल हमारा साथ निभाया और इस पुस्तक को पूर्ण किया और अतुलनीय भूमिका निभाई । आप सभी को दिल से शुक्रिया ।

धन्यवाद

1. Shubhanjali Nishad

Compiler

She is shubhanjali nishad she hailing from kanpur up. her passion is writing. ND her hobbies is reading books ND travelling. her aim is to achieve success in short time. She want to become a professional writer in his life.she completed 200+ anthology books as a co author nd contact with her through Gmail I'd nishadrock96@gmail.com insta I'd kanha_ki_laado

टूटा दिल

टूटा हुआ दिल लेके किस

तरह दूर जाऊं मै तुमसे

किया था जो प्यार हमने

तुमसे उसे अब अकेले

निभाऊं मैं कैसे हुई थी

क्या खता हमसे अब वो

गिले शिकवे मिलकर तुमसे

कुछ मिटाऊं मैं कैसे जो छोड़ा

है मोहब्बत के निशां रेत पर अब

उनपर जाकर अश्क बहाऊं मैं कैसे

जो लिखे हैं नाम हमने तुम्हारे संग में

उन नामों का वाजूद शाखाओं के पेड़

पर लिखे नामों को अकेले मिटाऊं मैं कैसे

अब तुम ही बताओ ये बेसहारा टूटा हुआ,

दिल ले जाकर दिखाऊं किसी को मै कैसे।

2. Priya Chopra

Her name is Priya Chopra.By profession she's an assistant professor,a writer and a Co-author of this splendid anthology.She has fond of writing since her childhood, she's the Co-author of other anthologies like Majestic Afternoon, Heightening Delirium, Mirror, Life and so on.Her write-ups are usually based on the attitude towards life apart of this she writes motivational and inspirational thoughts too.

Quarantine Life

Birds whisper to each other,

Hey! Pals let's sit together,

Let's enjoy the quarantine fun,

Let's be independent,

Let's talk about worldly puppets,

Let's ask them a question,

Are they enjoying while being caged?

Let's give them a sweet explanation,

We hope that they've understood the meaning of emotion,

Which was beyond of their notion,

Now they're bearing this unprecedented motion,

With the persistence of lockdown's promotion,

Neither corruption nor donation,

They've solely exhausted and wanna do supplication.

Ohh! Worldly beings, Almighty's wand did your character's correction,

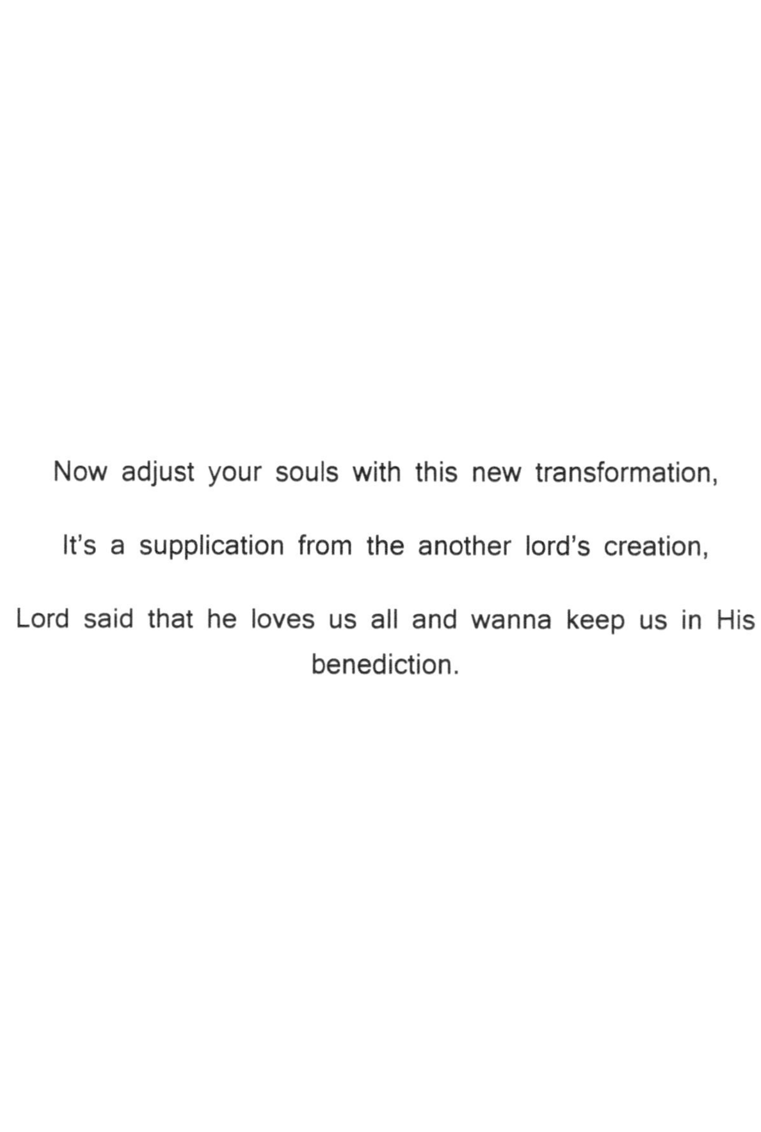

Now adjust your souls with this new transformation,

It's a supplication from the another lord's creation,

Lord said that he loves us all and wanna keep us in His benediction.

3. Lakshmi Priya.P

I'm a" Crow Tit".
This is Lakshmi Priya.P or Hope from Theni district,
Tamilnadu.
She is Pursuing Bsc Psychology.
Life is a chance not a choice.

Miserable Pain

Every morning makes me

To feel that I'm alone

Thinking that my eyes get wet

My Heart starts to feel

Miserable Pain

Even Air become My enemy

Nothing goes well

I'm living in hell

Without dieing

I don't where my life goes on

But I know my each day's are

Moving like a 1 year

Can't able to bear pain

My demon inside is shouting and

Making me a crazy!

4. NOOR TABASSUM

The name of the author is Noor Tabassum. Writing is her passion. She has participated in more than 300 anthologies as co author and has also written solo books called Sensibles and Twisted Firsts. She is a nature lover and loves to lead a simple life. She expresses all her feelings in her writings as she thinks it is the most powerful medium to communicate. She has won many writing competitions, and her articles have been published in many magazines too. She enjoys writing poems and short stories. Her stories have been published in the Times of India newspaper too. Her Instagram id is @noortabassumali123

BREAK UP

No squeezing of the heart is so painful,

No ache is so deep and hurtful,

When eyes rain blood and tears were stressful,

When loneliness is the only friend in the night direful,

When even the kind words pinch seeming harmful,

When eyes love to rain secluded so that no one can notice this sight awful,

It is break up which drains all the energy and makes us crazy for being loyal,

It may seem easy to advise,

All tell to move ahead because the partner did not deserve,

They say it is good to be away from a person toxic,

But no one can comprehend the pain flowing in the veins,

Hollowing the heart and increasing the pain,

No one looks good; no goodness feels excellent,

The pain caused by the sweetheart reigns.

They say time heals the pain,

But I think this is the only agony which increases with time,

And induces the feeling of hatred and jealousy,

Making everything related to love bitter and toxic,

And finally destroying oneself to the extent of seeing everything with doubt,

And hating lovers for their involvement in each other as they sprout,

Well, this is the effect of the break-up on a person who was once loved.

5. Manik Gupta

23 साल के मानिक गुप्ता जो की शामली , उत्तरप्रदेश के निवासी है । कार्य के सिलसिले में वो अभी गुरुग्राम में रहते है । वह पिछले एक साल से लिख रहे है । उन्हें अभी तक 10 से भी ज्यादा किताबों में रचनकार के रूप में योदान दिया है । और भी किताबों में अपनी रचनाएं प्रकाशित करना चाहते है ।

उसकी यादें

उसकी यादें मुझे सोने भी नहीं देती

न जाने क्यूँ है वो इतनी दूर मुझसे

मैंने तो तुम्हें रोमियो से भी ज्यादा चाहा है मेरी जूलियट

पर न जाने क्यूँ तुझको यकीन नहीं मुझपे

मिलने को बेताब हूँ पगली मैं तुझसे

पता नहीं वो सुनेहरा वक़्त कब आएगा

पर देख लेना जब भी वो वक़्त आएगा

दुनिया थम जाएगी और धड़कनें बढ़ जाएंगी

मिलने के लिए एक घण्टा पहले पहुँच कर इंतजार करूँगा

फिर सोच में डूबा रहूँगा की आखिर तुमसे क्या क्या बातें करूँगा

काम तो थोड़ा मुश्किल ही है

लड़कियों के मामले में थोड़ा कमज़ोर जो हूँ

पर टेंशन न लेना

उस दिन मैं बाज़ी मार ही लूंगा

बस प्लिज़ यूं सपनों में आ कर तो तंग न किया करो

आँख खुलने पर बड़ा दुख होता है

दुनिया की मुझे कोई परवाह नहीं

बस तुम मुझे समझते रहना

पहली बार मिलने के बाद चाहे जो भी हो

बस अपनी कुछ यादें छोड़ जाना

यादों संग ही वक़्त गुज़ार लूंगा मैं

बस तुम अपना ख्याल रखना और यूँही मुस्कुराते रहना

6. Nayan Datey

नयन दत्तये जो की पुणे महाराष्ट्र के निवासी हैं । वे एक छात्र है । इन्हें अपने जज़्बातों को शब्दों में पिरोकर लिखने का शोक है । इन्हें पुराने एवं नए गाने सुनना बहुत पसंद है ।

कोई मिला

बहुत वक़्त बिताने के बाद,

कोई ऐसा मिला था , जिससे न कोई शिकवा , न कोई गीला था,

मांगी दुआ खुदा की

साथ हमेशा बना रहे,

बदले में जवाब मिला

बिछड़ने के लिए तो मिला था

दर्दभरी ज़िन्दगी में भी

छुपा है राज़ है

उनके अंदर दम तोड़ती

अनसुनी आवाज़ है

खामोशी है जुबान पर

और सर पे उनके ताज है

बेवफा वो ही है

जिनपे हमको नाज़ है,

अबतक चुप थे हम

कुछ ऐसी हालत है

छोड़ गये है वो हमें

क्या खत्म हुए उनके जज़्बात है

ना जाने कब बितेगी

ये डरावनी सी रात है ।।

7. SANAT KUMAR MISHRA

He is Sanat kumar Mishra a boy dwelling in the 15th year of his life & studying in Class-10. He is a writer and a pretty well artist. He was born and brought up in cuttack, odisha. He feels immensely pleasured to write poems about emotions & upheavals in life. He entered the arena of literature not long before 4 years when he wrote his first poem in English.

TWO FACES OF A LOVELY COIN

Real Bliss of life lies in love makes

The heart beat with a rhythmic stakes;

Nourishes the soul of a lively plant,

Making his life like heaven with happy grants.

Instills a spirit of joy in the shattered parts,

Ignites the mind with strength for grief to depart.

Matures the growing seed of a plant into:

A well understood man with satisfaction to due.

But!!! Being duped with the flattering looks:

Got seized with the barbarous hooks;

Believing it as to be the bliss of life'-

Yet! Confronted a groaning deadly strife.

Amused by the monotonous tread-

Of the love, made the happy flowers shed.

Instilled a sense of high rage and anger,

Made the dwelling grievous and danger.

Pinned the delicate soul of life inside

& Hurt the heart with sad emotions beside.

Even Pained heavily by the swindling tides;

& Taunted the loving instict and cried.

Following the pensive grievous mourn-

Outcome a bright day of glorious sun:

With full of fun and blooming flowers,

Adorning a new fresh plant with success showers.

8. Kavitha Sridhar

कविता श्रीधर जी जो एक आईटी कंसलटेंट हैं और भारत मै ना रहने के बावजूद भी ये कविता लिखते हुए हिन्दी का मान कायम करते हुए अपना कविता पाठ शालीनता से करती है। यह कविता इसलिए लिखती है ताकि अपने विचारो को दुनिया के कोने तक पहुंचा सके और लोगो को प्रेरित कर सके।। यह हिंदी/उर्दू में फ्यूज़न पोएम लिखना पसंद करती है।
Youtube/Facebook/Instagram : #whenkavisriwrites

वह चाँद बन गए ...

तुम्हे हम चांद क्या कह गए..

तुम आसमान में ही बस गए...

जिंदगी को अंधेरा कर गए..

फिर उसमे नूर बिखरते रहे...

हमेशा कई तारो के बीच रहे..

पर किस तारे के तुम हो सके ...

कभी बे-वज़ूद कभी मुक़माल..

जब चाहा तब हुए न शमील...

तुम्हे हम चांद क्या कह गए..

तुम आसमान में ही बस गए...

9. Apeksha Khedkar

"14 साल की अपेक्षा खेड़कर , जो की पुणे की निवासी । वो अपने जज़्बातों को लिखकर जाहिर करना पसंद करती है ।"

दिल ने जिसे अपना

दिल ने जिसे अपना समझा

फिर चाहे उसने हमें कुछ भी नही समझा

दिल ने जिसके बिना रहना नहीं सीखा

फिर चाहे उसने हमें जीने ही नहीं दिया

दिल ने जिसे दिल में बसा लिया

फिर चाहे उसी ने दिल तोड़ दिया

टूटे हुए दिल से भी जिसे प्यार दिया

फिर चाहे उसने हमें नफरत के सिवा कुछ न दिया

दिल ने अपनी खुशियों के बदले जिसकी आबादी की मांगी है दुआ

फिर चाहे उसने हमें बर्बाद कर दिया

बार बार दिल उस पर निसार किया

बार बार जिसने दिल को दर्द दिया

यार उसने हमसे कोई रिश्ता नहीं रखा

फिर भी दिल ने जबरदस्ती उससे रिश्ता रख लिया

अब मे समझ गया कि खुद के सिवा कोई और साथ नही देता

और प्यार के सिवा कोई और दर्द नही देता |

10. Kamini Pradhan

कामिनी प्रधान , जो ग्राम पोस्ट आमगांव , शाखा - तमनार , जिला - रायगढ़ छत्तीसगढ़ से रहने वाली है, जो अभी एम.एस. सी रसायन शास्त्र में अध्ययनरत है । जो पढ़ने लिखने के अलावा संगीत में रुचि रखती है ।।

" ब्रेकअप "

ब्रेकअप नही करनी हमे और न ही दूर रहना है एक दूसरे से ,

प्यार करते हैं एक दूसरे से , जाती है दिल की हर आवाज उसके दिल तक ,

याद उसकी आती है , बिछड़ने का गम और आंखे नम हो जाती है ,

पानी बहुत कम पिया करते है मगर उसकी याद में तकिया गीला हो जाती है,

खामोश पल में भले ही शांति छाई रहती हैं मगर आखों में उसकी परछाई ,

हम चाहते है एक दूसरे से बात करना मगर बात नही होती,

बस याद कर लिया करते हैं और खुश हो जाया करते है ,

चाहते तो मुस्कुरा जाए उससे बात करके मगर आदत नही बना सकते ,

प्यार हुआ रब की मेहरबानी से , लकीरों में उसका नाम लिखना भूल गए ,

किस्मत ने ब्रेकअप कर रखा है हमारे प्यार पर ,

नही तो हमारी लाइफ में ब्रेकअप का नाम ही नहीं ।।

11. Har Deepansh Bahadur Sinha

He is Har Deepansh Bahadur Sinha .
He belongs to Lucknow,UP.
He is a research scholar of Oceanography and has
done masters in Geography from National Post
Graduate College.
Completed his schooling from Study Hall.
His hobbies are art , listening to music , cooking &
loads of driving. His interest areas are
Astronomy,Writing,Photography & Travelling a lot.

Devastating Love

The day I got betrayed

Heart beats got derailed,

Why you gave me such pain

My eyes turned into drain.

I was addicted to your presence

It's hard to digest your absence,

Literally I didn't have any idea of your act

But I loved you this was the fact.

I was supposed to think about you whole day

I thought our pair will slay,

The moment you left me my smile got lost

In my heart I felt and survived a blast.

It feels like I am drowning in a trench

Every seconds I am losing my strength,

You could have given us a pause

But you preferred to just run off.

Didn't know that she was pretending to be kind

She was my sunshine and today she made me blind,

It's hard to digest that you won't be my wife

But I beg you please return to me my life.

12. Vijay Singh Raj

विजय सिंह राज, उन्होंने हिंदी साहित्य में परा स्नातक किया है । वह पिछले 10 सालो से हिंदी में रचनाएं लिख रहे है ।उन्होंने हिंदी की विभिन्न विधाओं में रचनाएं की है उनकी कई रचनाएं और लेख विभिन्न पत्र पत्रिकाओं और समाचार पत्रों में प्रकाशित हो चुके है ।

बेवफा से वफा

जिसको हमने चाहा दिलों जान से,

वो किसी और की जान निकली |

दिखाये जिसने हमे जन्नत के सपने,

वो किसी और की दिलों जान निकली ||

वफा की हमने उससे हर दम,

उसे पाने के लिए |

हरदम दुवाओं में मांगा उसको,

उसने मन्नत भीं मांगी तो किसी और के लिए ||

दिल तोड़ना ही था तो बताते पहले,

हमने सपने भी देखे तो सिर्फ तेरे ही लिए |

टाइम पास करना ही था तो बताते पहले,

हमने तो दिल की चिरागो में उजाला किया था सिर्फ तेरे लिए ||

हम तो अनजान थे,

तेरी फितरत अब तक हमदम |

इतने रंग रूप तो गिरगट ने भी,

नही बदले होगे मेरे हमदम ||

अब भी मौका है तेरे पास,

साबित कर दे खुद को |

वर्ना तेरा नाम,

बेवफाओ में लिखना होगा ||

13. Emerald Reshma Reddithota

Emerald Reshma Reddithota is a Student, Writer, Travel Lover. She has published her works at different platforms and also in a local daily newspaper 'Cityline Hitavada' in youth zone column. She has also published her works in her college magazine 'The Hislopian' and also in her church magazine 'The Cathedral Messenger' which are both yearly and bi-yearly magazine respectively.

Why only love?

Why does only true and pure love suffer betrayal?

Why do people with pure hearts get nothing in return for their love?

Why and how people can cheat their loved ones?

Why do people suffer heartbreak because of their imperfections and flaws even with genuine and pure hearts?

Are imperfections bigger than love?

Why and how do people use beautiful emotion 'love' to use people for their selfish needs?

When this world will learn to value genuine and pure love?

14. Nithila Shri

Nithila Shri, 18 years old, is pursuing her graduation in engineering. She is an optimistic person who cherishes music and books to be the best part of her life. She considers writing as an opportunity to express her thoughts in simple words. This is her sixth book as a co-author. Besides being a co-author, she is also a singer.

BREAK UP

BREAK UP.... This is something that cannot be expressed in words. But still I attempt to share my opinions as I have also gone through break up because of unrequited love.

No one intentionally breaks up. There would be certain reasons behind this. But the broken people are pushed down to a situation where they cannot even think about those reasons because of depression.

Their mind is always clouded with memories of past where they and their loved ones used to cherish each other with immense joy and pleasure. Every promise they made turns out to lose it's value. The dream life which they wanted to live seems to end up as a dream itself. Life suddenly changes upside down. Finally the left ones are depression, anxiety, stress, sobbing etc.... I too came across these phases.

But finally I realised the reality of life and temporariness of people in it. If you overthink and take everything deep into your heart, you are the one who's going to be hurted. Let thousands of promises be made, but don't blindly believe anything. As time changes there are chances for the promises also to change.

At last , break up should not break everything in your life. It is necessary to come out of it. But believe me! The phase starting from break up to retrival of your self teaches you many worthy lessons for life. Cherish those lessons with grateful heart and live your life with immense joy and pleasure!

BREAK UP!

RISE UP!

GLOW UP!

15. Mrs.Gagneet Kaur Saluja

श्रीमती गागनीत कौर सलूजा जो की भोपाल की निवासी है ।
उनकी पैदाइश एवं पढ़ाई इंदौर में हुई । फिलहाल वो एक बेहतीन
गृहनी और दो बच्चों की माँ है ।
उन्होंने अपना स्तानक बी.कॉम में पूरा किया और कुछ वक़्त तक
उन्होंने प्रि स्कूल में शिक्षिका के रूप में भी काम किया। पढ़ना ,
गाने सुनना और छोटे छोटे पंक्तियों को संभाल कर एक जगह
रखना उन्हें बेहद पसंद है क्यूँकि यही उनके छोटे से दुनियां का
हिस्सा है । वो कहती है की अपने जज़्बातों को लिखकर व्यक्त
करना बहुत अच्छा लगता है । दिल को सुकून सा महसूस होता है
।

Instagram id - gagneetsaluja
Insta page- ankahey_eahsaas

• 58 •

मोहब्बत कैसे बयां करूँ

अनेक रूप इसके ,

कैसे मैं बयां करूं,

एक मां की हो या पिता की,

औलाद की हो या आशिक की,

लफ़्ज़ों में कैसे बयां करूं ।

प्यार हो तो है,

एहसास है,

दिलों में घर कर जाए,

वो जबात हैं।

रूठना मानना खेल मोहब्बत है,

पर दिलों से जुड़ना , दलों को जुड़ना,

ये नेमत उस रब की है,

सब अपने होते नहीं,

सबको अपना बनाना होता है,

दिलों में को आए दूरी ,

उसे मिलकर मिटाना होता है।

प्यार तो सबसे सबको होता है,

पर एहसास कहीं खो जाता है,

कौन अपना है ,

कौन पराया है,

इस उधेड़बुन में ,

अपना कही खो जाता है।

मोहब्बत के नाम अनेक,

मोहब्बत के रंग अनेक,

चढ़ जाए जो सब पर ये रंग,

सब हो जाएं एक

16. Syedah Hafiza Rabia Iqbal

Syedah Hafiza Rabia Iqbal, belongs to Pakistan. She's an artist, publishd writer, co-author, compiler and calligrapher as well, she has been participated in national and international writing contests. She has been completed her master in English and Urdu literature and linguistics as well. She's an animal lover and having deep affiliation with nature. She wants to spread peace and positivity and purpose of her writing is to reveal realities and highlights the social issues. Her favorite genre is poetry. She's a motivational speaker and by profession an English teacher.
@syedahbia

shrabiaiqbal@gmail.com

Feelings of Heart

"Heart is the most precious ornament in the world."

It makes you beautiful and loveable only in one way when you make it pure and free from all debris.

Heart isn't a dustbin that you put all your worries and anxiety in it, it's the most beautiful box in which we can collect our golden memories.

Everything in this world looks ugly after breaking but heart is the only one Who looks adorable after breaking, when it breaks it mends in so accurate way that we can then understand the realities of life, before it we were living in false realities, once in a life for our mental growth it's necessary to experience the pain, so we'll be enable to feel the hidden objects, unspoken words.

@syedahbia

17. Dhivya AL

She likes to write quotes and story's
She pursing her PG now
Co-author in many anthologies

My Feelings for Him

Oneday you will know my value!...

Oneday you will felt my love!....

Oneday you want me back!...

Oneday you will try to find me in others!...

Oneday you will hate yourself for broked me!..

Oneday you want to die for me!...

But that day my feelings for you only alive!...

Because I died on the day when you broke meJ

By left me!....

18. Gungun

She is gungun she hails from Assam. She is in class 7 . Her hobbies are reading , Dancing , Singing . She start writing in month of January 2020 . She want to be a writer and a CEO.

One

The night has a thousand eyes,

And that day but one !

Yet the night of the bright world dies ,

With the dying sun

The mind has a thousand eyes ,

And the heart but one

Yet the light of the whole life dies

When love is gone ~

19. Baivaw jha

Baivaw Jha is a well known Educator of Patna, Bihar. He also provides financial and legal Consultancy apart from that he has written many wonderful poetries. This is one of them.

तुम्हारे ख्यालों से फुर्सत

तुम्हारे ख्यालों से फुर्सत मिली है आज

आज फिर ये सुबह आशाओं वाली लग रही है

मन हल्का है, ना हीं कोई उम्मीद है ना ही अफसोस

ना ही तुम्हारी यादें खुशी दे रही है ना ही कोई ग़म

या कहूं तो आज तुम मुझे महसूस ही नहीं हो रही हो

टिक टिक करती घड़ी मुझे वक्त गुजरने का पैग़ाम दे रही है

मेरे मन में शोर नहीं है बस एक सन्नाटा है सुकून है

भले ही तुम आज हो नहीं पर कोई सिकन नहीं है

बस ये गुजरता पल एहसास दिला रहा है कि मैं जिंदा हूं।

20. Srija Sadhukhan

Srija Sadhukhan is studying BSc Biotechnology in Amity University Kolkata. Love to write poetry and a book worm too.

Break up

I was in love with you madly

You played with my feelings badly

You broke me and our relationship

From that day I broke my love grip.

When you again wanted to come back in my life

Now I don't have any love for you inspite

I held my own hands, I hugged my own arms

And I promised myself to be mine forever.

As I realize I will meet my best one

When I am in love with myself and all alone

I won't ever accept you and won't make that same mistake
ever

Self love is better than promising you to be your love
forever.

21. Rida Sultan

Rida Sultan loves writing creative content .she likes leading a simple life but in super creative way . Here is one of her most favourite writeup of all time .

MY ONLY ROLE MODEL

We love to follow, walk on the path and Sunnah of Prophet Muhammad (pbuh). We follow Him because there's a lot we can learn from Him. From Him, do we learn that the greatest sacrifice is to battle our own soul, to fight the evil within ourselves. From Him do we learn and understand that the best of the people are those who are most beneficial to others.

What a great and uncomparable personality He was! He used to feed the hungry, visit the sick person and free the captive if he/ she was unjustly confirmed. Despite the religion, He used to assist any person who was oppressed.

To Him do we follow, and we don't do evil to those who do evil to us, and we deal with them with forgiveness and kindness. His learnings are so beautiful and motivating :-
We learn from Him that we should not cause harm or respond to harm with harm. I've understood that it's better to remain silent than speak evil. And his words, O Prophet Muhammad, you were so great! You used to say that "An Arab has no superiority over a non-Arab and white man has no superiority over black man, nor a black man over white- except by piety and good actions." Yet in today's world we see so much conflict going on - regarding these topics. I wish All could follow the path of My Beloved Messenger Of Allah, Prophet Muhammad (pbuh).

By all means do I believe that whoever has faith and believes in The Lord and The Last Day will either speak good or remain silent .

If you notice, the teachings and sayings of Prophet Muhammad (pbuh) are connected to each one of our lives. We shall learn from Him so that we can lead a simple and happy life and proudly face the Lord rather than being ashamed.

22. Meera Gopalakrishnan

Meera Gopalakrishnan has been writing under the pen name Shruthi since 2018 when she first published her novel Seven Vows. She has also co authored 20 anthologies so far(15 in her pen name Shruthi,5 as Meera). Before becoming a writer, she was working in IT industry and used to analyze TV shows like Diya aur Baati Hum, Ek Hasina Thi, Siya Ke Ram, Beyhadh etc. She loves Indian mythology, culture and Indian history and interested in weaving stories around that. She has an active profile in Wattpad shruthiravi13 and her insta id is mira_g_pai.

Silence

They say silence is the language of the heart. True. The burning pyres were silent. But they told the stories of numerous families whose dreams were snatched untimely by the pandemic

The casket wrapped in tricolor was silent. But it carried the fighting spirit of a soldier who laid down his life to protect their motherland

The mud that buried the families underneath was silent. But the sight made each human realize the power of the nature that can make a thriving housing colony into just a mound of mud

The river that overflowed was silent. But as the water receded it carried with it the tears of the people who lost their near and dear ones in the flood.

Yes silence was the language of the heart. Silence was the language of feelings and it expressed itself in varied forms when faced with the ultimate truth of life that's death.

23. Aditi singh

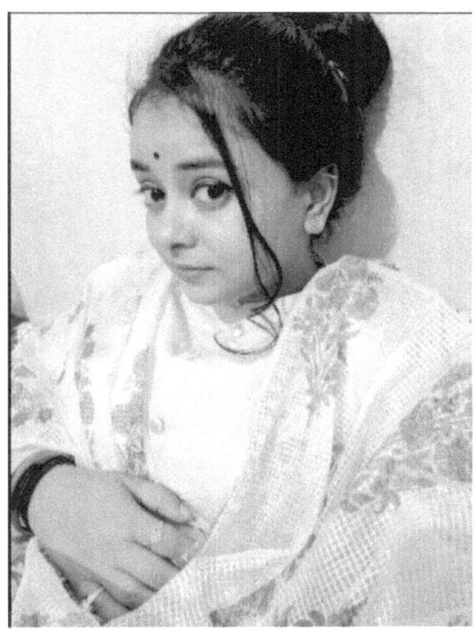

She is Aditi Singh Her date of birth is 17th of October. She belongs to Bihar Patna she Love music, Drawing, Writing...she is completed her masters in Mumbai as a digital marketer also completed ITI she is a botanist ,Digital Marketer, writer and she has works on Social media Like Fb, Insta, LinkedIn, Twitter and so on. She's Currently the Project head of a Ink Zone Publication.

She has a passion of writing she likes to inspired people by her writing skill and it's important for her to create the content "what the reader wants" she is compiler ....of books till date among which came in the top bestselling books on amazon/Google n co author in no. of books etc. catch her on Insta.aditisinghsh123

Dark side of Love

Love is all pain

In the event that you don't have a problem

How is that possible

To love somebody

Your careless

Is the best approach to

Discouragement

In the event that you track down it

You hurt in view of the difficulty

Bring one another

Unending pain

It's gone at this point

You can follow

What's more, on the off chance that you lose it?

Your tears and disappointments

Is the shadow of life

Trust in genuine affection

Develop inside you

Inside is

Presently full with openings

24. Gaytri Manchanda

Gaytri manchanda was born & brought up in delhi .
Gaytri is currently persuing her graduation from delhi
university , she's fluent in 3 languages . Gaytri has
compiled 3 books & has her words in 20+ anthologies
. For her writing is not a job it's the most purest form
of expressing feelings & thoughts .
For more you can check her instagram
@the.introvert.pens

Toxic

Ehh.. You're Toxic

You cage them ? Epicc !

Excuses , damn I was just sick

That made my anxiety kick

You should die

But why ?

Anyways I'll try

Hope this wasn't a lie

You're death dealing

Sorry I thought you were healing

He looked at the ceiling

I asked , How are you feeling ?

Hollow he said

Even I feel dead

Well you go ahead

Let it all be unsaid

25. Salma khan

सलमा खान इंदौर की निवासी है । उन्हें अपना स्नातक की पढ़ाई देवी अहिल्या विश्वविध्यालया इंदौर से किया है । उन्हें लिखना , पढ़ना , चित्रकला , गायिका भी है । उन्होंने अक्टूबर 2021 से अपनी रचनाओं को सह लेखिका के तौर पर किताबों में प्रकाशित कर चुकी है ।

टूटे दिल के ज़ज़बात

तुमने खुद ही फैसला कर लिया मुझसे दूर जाने का...

एक बार अपने दिल की धड़कनों से भी पुछ लेते हैं....तुम्हे जवाब मिल
जाता मेरी धड़कनो का...

बहुत अकेली हो गई हूं तुम्हारे दूर जाने के बाद...

अब मन नहीं करता फिर से मुस्कुराने का..

जबसे तुम दूर हुए हो...

सारा जहांन विरान सा लगता है...

आज भी मेरे दिल की डायरी में एक पेज मोड रखा है...

उस पेज में लिखे हर किससे को बस खुद से जोड़ा रखा है..

कैसे भूल जाऊ तुम्हे..

तुम मेरी पहली और आखिरी मोहब्बत हो...

इन वादियों में तलाश रही हूं खुद को...

मिल जाउ कहीं अगर तो , मुझे खुद से ही कुछ सवाल करना है...

वादा किया था उसने उमर भर साथ निभाऊंगा...

बेवफा नहीं है वो, मुझसे दूर जाने की भी उसकी जरूर कोई वजाह रही
होगी .....

तुम कुछ नहीं जानते....आज भी अंजान हो तुम...

मेरी मुस्कान में छुपे हुए हर दर्द से...

तुम्हारी हर बात मुझे बार-बार याद आती है..

करू लाख कोशीशें फिर भी नहीं भुलाई जाती है..

सुना है जो ख्वाहिशें अधूरी रह जाती है...

वो हमें जिंदगी भर बहुत तड़पाती है...

तेरा हाथ यू छुटने लगा मेरे हाथो से...

जैसे मेरे जिस्म से मेरी रूह जा रही हो...

मेरी आंखे आज भी तरस्ती है....

तेरी आँखों में वो पहले

जैसी मोहब्बत देखने के लिए....

एक सवाल है, जबाब देना तुम सच्चा...

क्या मिला तुम्हें, हमसे भी कोई अच्छा...

26. Sanju Agarwal

He is Sanju Agarwal. He lives in bihar and he complete his study. He loves to write story, Poem and shayari.He also work in mt Kenya Times Paper . He is a helpful person. He is a founder of publication

I could ask

I could ask you to stay,

But there's really nothing left to say.

This breakup has been emotional and long,

But I know I'm strong.

I guess we naturally grew apart,

But it still hurts in my heart.

We went days without speaking or sending a text,

And I could only wonder what was next.

There were times we couldn't look each other in the eye.

How did we get this far, and why did something so special
have to die?

As I write this, memories flood me.

They remind of all we used to be.

Even when things were bad, I never thought this
relationship would end.

Our broken hearts I thought we could mend.

Now you've left without a goodbye.

I've got no energy to even cry.

I knew it was over when we started doing things on our own.

You got so distant and I was alone.

I tried getting you to notice that I was still there,

But you made up your mind and didn't care.

There are many nights when you're all that's on my mind.

I hope happiness is what you find.

There are days when I just can't get out of bed.

But "try" is what you always said.

So every day I try to put on a smile.

Even if it's not a real one for a while.

We were together for so many years, so do you ever shed tears?

I know I've got to let you go,

And someday I will,

But mixed emotions are what I feel.

We both made our fair share of mistakes.

It feels like I'm drowning in sadness, anger, and resentment, all in different lakes.

I honestly wish you nothing but the best

As my strength and endurance is put to the test.

27. Ramyaa K

Ms K. Ramyaa completed her 12th grade and getting ready for her entry in Medical field. A girl who never afraid to try new things, she always try to keep her busy by trying new things like hand crafts, drawings , writings and so on. She already published her debut book as a Co- author. In the world of expecting motivation from outside, she is the one who try to made herself as motivation for others. Be positive at any stage of life is her motto. And her favourite quote " Treat everything equal though it is good or bad".

Strong Fibre but Easily Broken

Love yourself!

Allow yourself for further more!

You won't get bore;

Create the strong you

Nothing can broke you;

Allow yourself for further more!

Go with the flow

You will grow;

Because you will shine

Wherever you go

And, whatever you do;

Allow yourself for further more!

It's a chapter

Not the novel;

If you think, you can make you;

If you think, that can't broke you hardly;

Love yourself!

Allow yourself for further more!

Hurting is easy but healing is difficult;

Take feelings as pill to build the best version;

Be the machine of converting negativity to positive;

Love yourself!

Allow yourself for further more!

Heart is made up of strong muscular fibre but it get easily
broken by hurt;

Think once before doing heart has

H "EAR" T to listen.

Love yourself!

Allow yourself for further more!

If you give the correct things to the

H "EAR" T,

It will make your life HE "ART" .

Take a "MIN" and take correct "D" ecision.

(MIND)

It "H" append, "EAR" listen, and finally,

"T" houghts makes life beautiful.

(HEART).

28. Aneesh Dey

Aneesh Dey is a just a student who is trying to explore his creative side through writing. He had always lived up to the words " it won't end, if I didn't made it". He is a unique person with a simple vision of the world.

I have taken chances

I have taken chances

Even Reused faith

With stiffness I have recovered

And nothing to wait

After all this years,

Now I don't have any fears

In time my mind is clear

I have stopped it all, dried up my tears

I have broken my heart

It's not for something to be cared about

In exchange it changed me around

All this big world to live for

But I'll consider it to be gone for

29. Rohiaya Intan Hia

Rohiaya Intan Hia is a Co-author and Compiler from Bangladesh. She's written in more than 90 anthologies. Intan loves to present her thoughts through her write-ups. She also enjoys sketching and painting.

COLD DECEMBER

Look back

Long road

A never-to-return place, left alone

Promises & dreams lying down like dry leaves

A common name where we came from

Done and dusted, became so random

But here we are acting just fine as usual

It hurts, it matters

But we don't matter anymore

Were supposed to be loved

Then why we hate each other?

Broke up just to feel a little better

But ended up in cold December

Love no longer exits

As lover's favourite playlist

Tearing up in a lonely bedroom

Where love no longer lives.

30. Anita Rohlan

अनिता रोहलन (आराध्यापरी)का जन्म नागौर के जिले लाछड़ी गाँव
में हुआ, इन्होंने बी.ए की पढाई श्रीमती मोहरी देवी तापड़िया कन्या
महाविद्यालय जसवनतगढ ,लाइन्नूँ से की,इन्हे खेल में भी रूचि है
इन्होंने कराटे मे रेड बेल्ट व ताईकावानडो यलो बेल्ट प्राप्त किया
है इन्हे गानो के बोल लिखना भी बेहद पसन्द है इन्हे नृत्य व
योगा मे भी बेहद रूचि है यह प्रकृति प्रेमी है इन्हे लिखना बेहद
पसन्द है पर यह इसे सामाजिक बदलाव का सशक्त माध्यम

मानती है इनकी 60 पुस्तकों मे कविताएँ प्रकाशित हो चुकी है

काश तू मेरा होता

काश तू मेरा होता __

अपना हर दर्द बया करती तुमसे

अपने हर एहसास मे रखती तुम्हे

काश!तू मेरा होता

तेरी बेइन्तहा मोहब्बत इतनी ही थी मेरे लिए

तेरी झूठी वफा को समझ न पाये हम

काश ! तू मेरा होता

अब अगर नही भी हो तो कौनसा तूफान आ गया

जिनके पास हो तुम

उन्होने कौनसे सितारे जमीन पे ला दिये

तुम रखना अपना एटीट्यूड अपने पास

अगर तुम किसी और के दिवाने हो

तो हम कौनसे तुमसे पहले सिंगल थे ।।